Prelude to Love: A Poetic Journey to Finding Love

This book is dedicated to my "higher self". I was stuck in the lower me for so long, yet I grew to meet you with confidence and perseverance.

Thank God for giving me the hard lessons needed to fulfil this journey. This book is years in the making, doubts and fears kept me from producing my soul's work. I thank God for breaking me down and transforming me into my power to finally publish my first book. This journey is aligned with my life's purpose; I always felt I needed to share my journey in hopes to help other women on their quest to self-exploration and love. Thank you to everyone who always asked when my book was coming out, and motivated me to get my work done. To my dear friends and family who were there from day one, y'all are the real MVP's and I will forever cherish your support and love for me. Thank you, mom, you never gave up on me and still motivated me, even when I was in my darkest hours. Your prayers never ceased for me and your love for me is so unconditional. You are loved and appreciated, thank you for trying your best to be an awesome supportive mother. To the Ying to my Yang, Sana Atirah, thank you for always being my spiritual sister, prayer partner, confidant, awesome cousin and being down to pray with me any time of day or night. Also, thank you for continuously allowing me to read my poems aloud to you or send to you randomly; your response was always "deep" (LOL- insider joke). To my friend Diamond, thank you for your motivation and support, your excitement for my book gave me the boost of confidence to get this out without any doubts. K.R. Copeland, thank you for showing me my greatest potential in my writing and never letting me lose my integrity in it as well. You Rock! Malcolm Xavier, your patience with me and my demands were always appreciated. I know I drove you insane with my constant changes to perfection, but through the annoyance, you always stayed professional and worked hard until we got what I loved! Special shout out to Lyric Poetic, Angela Mull and Tionna Smalls for being awesome mentors in my life, sharing wisdom and always uplifting women. Last but not least, thank you to my audience reading this book, may my journey inspire you to fill up your own cup, pour it into yourself and love with all of your heart.

Table of Contents

Intro: Lessons Learned

I've learned so much about love. I've learned that love is within ourselves, but we must learn to be patient, forgiving and understanding of ourselves. I prayed constantly to my higher being about selflove. It was never an overnight sensation, but it is and always will be a work in progress. Like most of us, I endured lots of emotional trauma, depression, PTSD, and a phobia of receiving and being in love. I learned through finding the "new" me that the 5 people you surround yourself with the most is usually a direct reflection of you, good or bad. I like to think of my closest friends/ fam as my tribe, they help cultivate a good or bad day, positive or negative attitude. I can recall one of my favorite inspirational Youtubers, Ralph Smart mention that "Your vibe attracts your tribe". Most people know the other phrase "Misery loves company", both are accurate either way. I am blessed to have a few amazing friends and family who are uplifting, motivating, supportive, ambitious and who exudes positive vibes.

They say be careful what you ask for because you just may receive it. I remember praying and asking God to remove any toxic and negative people from my life and replace them with positive beings. Slowly but surely, peacefully and quietly, friends who I thought would always remain in my life began to disperse. My life became more peaceful though I was so dependent on those friends. I missed them indeed, but deep down I knew that God had to remove me from that circle so I can grow. I still have love for them, just from a far. Not everyone is meant to be in your life forever, some people are meant to be there for a season to teach you a lesson from the universe. I learned over time that you can be in a poisonous relationship or friendship and be completely unaware of it. When you don't value your worth it's hard to see anything other than what's in front of you. It is a crippling mindset that stays until the you actually stop, realize, and take action to better your mental and emotional state.

I wasn't sure who or where to turn to when I had suicidal thoughts and isolated myself from the world.

I ended up googling and found a therapist that I dealt with on and off for about 4 years or so. I was desperate and needed to find a non-biased person to speak to and get perspective from to help me organize my thoughts and feelings. It was a great experience for me, but no it didn't stop my depression or my PTSD. I even spent money on this amazing life and career coach, who literally gave me the best advice and helped me on my career path. It helped but I wasn't willing to open up and take heed to everything. I was still on a path of self-destruction while still trying to find myself. I had to stop, look within and when I couldn't stand to look at myself or deal with myself, I swear the universe placed situations and people in my life so that I was forced to. It's not easy looking into your baggage while it's still weighing heavy on your shoulders. But in order to heal yourself, you must forgive yourself, embrace yourself, and love on yourself. Everyone's journey to self-love is different, but we all have to put in the "work", as Iyanla would say. Poetry is my main outlet of expressing my feelings of doubt, anger, hurt, unrequited love and also my expression for learning to love myself.

The signs or the red flags are always in front of our face, but we choose to ignore them for the sake of love or lack thereof. What did I believe love was? A co-dependent situation covered with toxicity that leaves the soul withering for help. "The heart wants what the heart wants", I was once told. Well I guess my heart needed my love more than anyone else's who sucked my energy dry. I had to let go of them and let go of my old self to finally evolve. Love is a light filled within the soul, sometimes that light is dim or is non-existent until we are ready to start our journey of self-love. Love is a light that illuminates every positive vibration and releases endorphins. That light may not always be lit, but when it is and we work hard on it being so, it's better than sex, a cerebral foreplay.

Preface

I was blind. Not blind in the sense of Ray or Stevie, but rather in the sense of ignoring the signs. I fell for what I thought he could be. My expectations of him exceeded his abilities. He was doing only what he knew. Broken hearts came together in time of just want and rebound. Years of frustration led us nowhere. His hiatuses proved he had no intentions to be what my poetry has once mentioned. Homeyloverfriend, this title has officially come to an end. My infatuations are now gone, my heart was never in use, he suppressed my appetite and fueled my libido. He was the only one I ran back to when shit hit the fan and stress consumed my life. But he took me on a high just to bring me right back down. A rollercoaster ride on his mysterious spell over me. I finally broke the strong karmic bond that had us connected for so long. I deserved better so I went and found myself, she was hidden beneath the bed of lies she laid on.

So many mistakes needed to be forgiven for, but she accepted me for me and loved me endlessly. Sometimes it gets lonely, but there's no void that music, poetry and meditation can't fill. I cared for him and with doing that I neglected self-care. Loving me has been such a beautiful transformation. I learned that it can intimidate people, and it doesn't need to be spoken, it shines from within. I also learned that it's a process and something that has to be worked on daily. Life is always full of challenges, then there's media images of what you should look like and who you should be, neglecting the inner core of self-love. Self-love doesn't ask for validation from any outside source. Self-love is a journey and sometimes insecurities arise within it. We are all not without flaws, our flaws make us each unique. No one genius is alike. I wrote this book to prove the power I have inside still exists. I wrote this book to release my emotions, pain and transformation into the world. This is for all of the young girls and to the women that they are becoming. To let them know that the love they are so eagerly trying to find within everyone else is right within themselves. This is for my sisters, my real friends who I have seen repeatedly suffer, go through trials and tribulations just to be accepted by a man or by society. Most importantly, this is for Myself, so that I am reminded not to turn back down that dark and desperate road again. This is for LOVE! Not mediocre love, not selfish love, not let's pretend love, but for the Love that the universe has finally let shine in my life---Real Love.

Because pure hearts will always be blessed and never be lonely.

Chapter 1: A Four-Letter Word

What is hope good for?

A means of frustration,

I don't want hope, it disappoints my ego.

I don't want to dream, for it may defer

Take me to reality, I want to live life as it is---in its truth.

Love?

Lord, what is this I constantly crave for?

Why does it make me mad and sad?

As I go after my prey, and through them I seek.

But I seem to never find what was missing from me in the first place.

So my heart turns iceberg from everyone who had a chance to make it melt.

Can no longer force the matters that may not be.

Crooked notions of what love should be.

I cry silently looking towards the sky,

Hoping one day you will remove this disguise.

So I may walk into it and indulge undoubtedly.

If only it were that simple,

I could give myself away down an aisle full of rose petals and an audience of smiles.

But what have I gained from all the heartaches and breaks?

But busted memories of what I thought it could be.

Holding on to the potential, knowing in the end I will miss them.

Eyes turn blind from the lies told to me.

But I awake knowing it wasn't meant to be.

But what is meant to be?

Living in the moment only makes it die slowly.

Facing the naked truth, like Eve in the Garden of Eden.

Snake bit me twice, and it's my fault.

Still looking at potential rather than reality.

It's still a warped sense, living off a fantasy.

No happy ending in sight though.

So I flip through fictitious memories,

Trying to embed in my brain that it will work this time around.

I was wrong again and I grew strong again.

How much stronger can I get?

How much more can I take?

When will I learn?

The same lesson being taught repetitively.

Same results, a bed full of lonely.

Feeling Forever

It's deeper than oceans and seas,

Never seems to hit rock bottom,

Because it's always afloat

The tides are high and we immerse in its intimate showers
Never letting the waves bring us ashore to dry.

Somewhere far enough that they can't see,

They're only left with assumptions of where they think we
could be

Between you and I we keep,

The truth shoved in a closet.

Falling in love with our reality When we swim, we swim
deep, Making a Hallmark of memories.

Blissful indulgence,

Tastes of cotton candy on a summer beach.

So much fun, so much passion, so intense, but yet so sweet.

What we got is like a full moon in the midnight skies. And when it dies, like a phoenix we rise.

Sherlock couldn't even conclude our story

An enigma,

But it's never too hard for us

A connection beyond the physical

Words never needed to be spoken, Knowing each other's mental and spiritual.

Never mistaking one another's energy.

Pure euphoria, never wanting to leave.

Our days are numbered so we live each one filled with electricity.

The fire that burns within,

Nirvana,

Beautiful chaos,

Two crazies against the world

Passing the time with wet kisses,

An audience is all that's missing

Bouquets of calla lilies ,

Smiles of acceptance,

Champagne flutes clinking,

Roses are meant to die,

Feed love food for thought,

Watch it nourish longer than its expiration. cvc

We never lost ourselves,

We just grew an extension of our hearts.

It shall remain even when we're apart.

A karmic bond,

The universe is in awe

We conquered it all, we came and we saw.

No one knows how this will end,

But the possibilities are infinite.

Jazzy Sull said "forever doesn't last",

So we'll be together each day until this thing dies.

La Flora

You're like a flower that only grows in the winter.

White Casablanca lily, standing bold against the snow.

So awkwardly beautiful.

You blossom in this cold climate and still somehow are able to give off heat.

They'll never see how special you are through the whiteness of the snow.

You stick out like a sore thumb from what I can see.

Beautifully captured by the sunlight.

I love to water your roots.

Knowing I can stimulate your mind.

It's a world that's made for you and I.

No one will ever know how deep this can be.

Without a simple touch, or words being said,

We feel each other's energy and my soul is content.

With the love in your heart that's been transferred into my own.

The biggest secret shared between us.

Evenly yoked in every way possible.

I see you for exactly who you are and I love every minute of your being

I never knew what real love was.

Until God showed me his love for me and in appreciating that he blessed me with another example within you.

I am here to bask in these feelings graciously and return them unto you.

You're my prayer that's finally been answered.

God saw fit that your pieces fit my puzzle so effortlessly.

You are my beloved friend; you love me for me.

Despite my craziness and insecurities. Accept me, flaws and all.

You keep me on my toes,

Soften me up when I want to be cold as ice.

Your smile is a thousand words left unsaid, but read perfectly.

Love in A Hopeless Place

The rain leaks through my bedroom ceiling.

Falling into a pot of wondrous hollowness.

The sound clashes with my REM sleep.

So I awake listening to its bold introduction. Flooding out my thoughts,

Only to concentrate on the sounds of its

boisterous ego.

It's one hell of a night,

The streets wash away dirt and fall silent

from the lack of people on the scene.

See.SZA.Run in my background, a dark mood, got me reminiscing.

I just want your kiss, place it on the wound you opened. Left without warning, now I'm high upon you, Wanting you like Eve wanted forbidden fruit.

There's just something about it, something about you. You're like the polyphenols in my loose leaf green tea.

Protecting me against the damage caused by free radicals.

But You can't save me from myself , my extremity is what makes me.

I was never ashamed of me, or even you,

I walk heels high and head in clouds unbothered by the masses against us.

Me and you against it all,

Neteru, I am queen, I can save you,

Save us, I am beauty, I am complex, I am strength, I am love.

I can't love you; I refuse. But fuck it,

Can't fight it, kismet. Your eyes tell it all,

My intuition loud and clear.

Ignoring what was meant,

I always wanted to fly so high,

But fear of falling always kept it a fantasy.

If only you could catapult me, propel me to the winds and maybe I

can believe.

Only fairytales have happily ever after endings.

So, if I go, I will go with dignity.

Hand in hand, they will remember when we,

When I reach heaven, will you still remember me?

Remember me for who I was, not who I am

I was a peaceful warrior,

Quick to anger, slow to love.

These clouds are fuzzy,

I can't see,

blinded as I drift into ecstasy.

Now I see what Eve has been saying all along.

I am not myself, I am different with you.

You make me feel with an intensity I never thought I could discover.

I opened my eyes and let go of your hand,

And that was the first time I ever felt freedom. When you loved me enough to let me go.

X-Factor

Distant kisses left me a tear away from lonely.

I wanted you completely,

But you couldn't love me for all of my crazy.

Abandoned,

After your bended knee of future promises.

Was once all I wanted,

The circle of love was missing,

Just like the heart.

You saved me from us,

Pacified me with endless reminders of why we weren't meant to be.

Only you could be the remedy to my misery.

But you never understood how much you meant to me.

I will never be good at saying goodbyes.

So I wrap myself in a blanket of lies.

Hoping someday you will return to me, because I lost my key.

You're the only one who can open up this deadbolt heart.

Cuz' with them I got on my shield,

Padlocks, chains, icebox---cold.

I put my all into you, for you to just segregate our love forever.

Are you sure?

Questions go unanswered,

And the spirit of our love floats out of my bedroom door.

Wails of agony, melancholy from your absence.

Faded pictures left in the depths of my closet along with our skeletons.

Possessions you gave me no longer have value, but I try to hang on to you.

I hold on to things that made us.

Time hasn't visited me as of yet,

So my wounds are wide open,

Sitting here wishing and hoping.

But in the end you left me with nothing.

My womb was ready for your seed,

Something I never thought I would want or even need.

Talks of our unborn having your big brown eyes and skin blessed with cocoa pigments of melanin.

Never knew love like this,

You gave me reassurance,

I had high hopes for us,

When it really was none for us.

All of the options on the table, but results left us parting ways.

I needed more time, another chance, one more day, just an hour.

To get clarity, better yet closure from it all.

One year of my life gone in one second.

Seasons changed, just like you,

When you said you needed space.

Alarms gone off,

Suffocations of an overzealous lover.

There were no gray areas with me,

I gave my all, my heart was never mediocre.

Infatuations of the white picket fence had me trapped in awe of us.

No back up plan, as if this was the law for us.

Shattered glass of broken memories,

Taste of bittuh on my tongue,

But in the end this is good for me.

Chapter 2: Homeyloverfriend

Come to me,

Like a night whisper, My body is calling.

You're so close, yet so far.

I need to get in touch with you,

Out of sight, out of mind---

Still on my mind,

Out of time,

Rest assured,

Wanting more,

Frustrations.

With You

I'll stay on this ride with you,

More than just a cheap thrill,

A constant reminder of how you really feel.

Never been the one to ride more than once continuously,

Hop on, hop off,

Next,

Simple motif.

I'm awaiting the climax,

screaming all the way from the pits,

Tears of joy,

down my cheeks, bittersweet on the tongue.

There's something about you,

That makes me unafraid to follow you,

where the doors are open in the dark.

No sight, I can finally feel again.

These vibrations send me through,

cosmic euphoria when I'm with you.

Black Stallion

Mine,

As the moonlight glows through my window pane,

Your eyes pierce through the bitter parts of me and finds its way into its sweet goodness.

I stare into the darkness of your pupils,

Trying to interpret your disposition

But you won't let me fathom it

Instead you softly place warm wet kisses,

on my neck,

Inviting me into your forbidden ecstasy.

With every kiss from head to toe, you show me how much I'm wanted.

I submit to your dominance, and let you open the door that's always been shut.

With every stroke, our sensation provides good vibrations and we feel each other's

energies release into the air of possibilities.

Corresponding only by loud moans, grunts and occasional mumbles under the heat of our breaths.

We go deep, and our positions are ever changing.

It's the unpredictable rhythm to the melody of our favorite love song.

You show me so many ways to be taken into the wild.

Tears roll down my cheeks, this is no emotional fit.

But dammit this is something to be reckoned with.

Never missing an inch of my body to touch, cradle or kiss.

Because selfless measures keep me in awe, keep me coming until I beg for more.

Followed by uncontrollable shivers and speechless afterthoughts.

Tasting my love to the very last drop, fearless and strong,

You are KING,

This sinful delight.

With our bodies we master the art,

Words unspoken, through every breath you exhale.

Hands around my neck, as I yell, sweet vicinities into these four walls and beyond.

Pain never felt so damn good, thrusting harder into the wees of the morning.

The levees break, a fountain of love.

Biting and holding tight,

I turn back and wait for you.

Instead you lick my face and lips,

Practice makes perfect.

Got my body singing "I'm a recovering undercover over lover" like Badu.

Want you so bad, that I hate you.

Then we share ourselves again and I love you.

For just one night only, I could live in this dream.

But then noon strikes and we wake up to our reality.

Unlike Cinderella, I only leave behind my sweet scent upon your face.

Daydreaming about what we just did,

This is lust, this is us, it's a must, I may bust, so we go nuts.

How could we ever forget?

It's hard for us to ever admit,

We weren't even meant for this

But hearts grow fonder each time we kiss.

Memories of what we did mar my mind,

Eyes closed, body paralyzed,

Shivering from the thought of your wet kisses going

down my spine.

Never wanting to stop, calling out for one more time

times three and you know just what I need.

Conversations on your chest, cuddles with you are

always the best.

I kiss your nice full lips and you lick my face as an

appreciation of my beauty.

I smile, we laugh

You stare, I drift away.

Wild Thing

Me,

No sleep,

Cravings of a wild beast, Wanting him here.

Need to get this off, before I go off.

Distances,

Makes me want him more.

Come to me,

Make me roar.

Passions of a peaceful warrior,

His eyes tell its soul.

Never wanting to let go,

this hold he has.

Dark but so full of light.

Unspeakable pleasures,

Bounded by moonlights of expressions.

His love howls to the moon.

Ninth cloud,

Seen with every stroke.

Shows me what he's afraid to say.

Loud and clear,

He loves,

No boundaries of how far he takes us.

Magical rides on unicorns,

Merry-go-round,

Dizzy spells,

Sensational,

Euphoria.

Only with him.

I found his heart hidden,

Beneath the castle he built,

He crowned me,

I accepted,

Imperfections of a perfect lover.

Our Connection is raw and real,

Saved by the sarcasms of platitudes.

I laugh all the way through.

Never wanting more than what it is,

Can't take another disappointment.

Afraid to feel, done with fantasies that never come into fruition.

So I let everything ride, on cruise control.

A different deck of cards and I'm playing wisely.

I got a winning hand, but I'm no fool, killing him softly....pokerface.

Ghost

Us,

Why should I persist?

Knowing that this thing I had in my head of us, will never exist.

Figure of my imagination,

Like a faded kiss,

A few weeks old,

Stained on my lips, engraved in my heart and on my mind.

Awaiting a new love,

But now so over it, maybe even you too.

There's no reciprocation, so let's stop this communication.

My energy is no longer in your direction,

In a new headspace, it was myself that I neglected

Now when you call, "Sorry, I'm busy" it gets rejected.

Filed your number under "unavailable", just like the emotions I tried to locate from you.

I deserve better, times ten.

Wasted my cape on someone who ain't tryna be saved,
Dusted it off and embraced myself.

Smiling at the "S" my heart now carries,

Self-care, is not selfish.

So before I chuck these deuces, Just know "it's not you, it's me".

It's me who wants more than what you can ever give,

I won't compromise my worth any longer.

So just like your love,

I'm disappearing.

You came through like a soft whisper,

Felt you near, slowly looked up to see.

The cool energy that was presented to me.

Captivated by your originality.

Leaped into your arms,

Something about the way you held me.

Chapter 3: Free

I am free,

Of the hold put on me,

No more addictions,

God rid me of your filth

And forgave me for giving you,

A sacred part of me.

What I thought was bound to blossom,

Only turned out to be weeds in a yard of worthless
dirt, No substance.

I won't allow myself to make the same mistake.

I almost got pulled into your charming ways,

But I caught myself before I drowned face down in
your sin.

Knelt down in prayer, as I repent—remember.

We built our castle in a day, It didn't withstand the
wind.

Made of sand.

It fell,

The inevitable.

Queen

Her soul dances,

happily to the unmatched rhythm.

Baring all,

Trying it all.

Unboxed,

Untamed, Never giving in.

Death to her old self.

Phoenix,

Proud and confident.

Smiles,

Laughter, Risks,

Unpretentious.

No judgement,

No pain,

No tears,

No fears

No shadows lurking from the past.

Unapologetic,

For she is free.

Heart open,

Listening to intuition,

Living for herself, No one else,

Selfish love of self.

A higher source,

Who loves unconditionally.

Peace,

Love,

Tranquility,

Serene.

Thoughts of positivity,

Dreams of adequacy,

Wife,

Home,

Child,

Career, Zen.

She wants all,

No limit,

God's child,

Never without,

Prayers never ending,

Answered in time.

He hasn't forgotten,

She hasn't given in,

She still believes,

Faith unwavered.

She sees the unseen,

Fruition,

Labor of love.

She falls deep,

Sleeves exposed,

She gives wisely.

She craves,

Showers of intimacy.

To feel,

To know,

To dare,

 To see,

Love.

She lives,

She becomes,

She is,

I.

Farewell

I left you at sea,

No longer wanting to be bound by unknown waters.

I am mother earth and this is where I shall reside.

Nature is my calling,

Blowing passed the trees that keeps me stuck.

Your waters became too deep, a sea full of agony.

The salt burned my soul,

Waves of unpredictability.

I thought this cool barrier of life would be serenity.

Wishful thinking had me going,

I lost myself between the tides.

Tried to stay afloat,

But your harsh waters kept pulling me further away from shore.

Your love became unsure, so I became distant.

Your love had me trapped like a tsunami, a whirlwind of unspoken emotions.

Drowning my heart into the bottom of the pit.

Feeding it to the scavengers, each

cringing moment aching my soul.

Never came to its rescue; just stared upon the reflection of the waters.

Narcissism got the best of you, pride cometh before fall.

But my love was always stronger than pride.

Compromising was never your thing.

Sacrifices to keep you near, rotten by my subservient manners.

Loving you was an atomic bomb, Tick, tock my patience goes.

Now I rest ashore,

Birds chirping and singing in the trees,

Bees making hives of honey,

Leaves growing on branches,

Sand clings to my feet,

Footprints trailing my way home,

Your pheromones still in the air, on my skin trying to reel me back in.

But I refuse,

Never looking back,

Instead to what's ahead of me.

Sun beams down and caresses my skin as it glows.

A smile creeps upon my face,

As satisfaction nears,

Total relief,

Comforted by living creatures,

Forgetting my past along the shoreline,

No rearview in sight,

No wading in the water for you to ride the wave.

Instead I wave,

Goodbye to your tides.

We drift apart like the red sea. But baby, I'm going green.

Packing

Stagnant, for fear has taken me in its wings.

A closet full of skeletons and I still can't seem to empty out anything.

Mind consumed with doubt

In my room, dark clouds overshadows

The storm is brewing inside, but I refuse to let my eyes bring tears.

For the rain has been here forever.

Bright colored walls full of vibrancy, but within its hollowness whispers the tragedies its held.

A safe haven within a nightmare

The only place where a mustard seed of peace can be found.

Holding on to the lovers, the love, the hate, the fights, the heartaches, the tears, the smiles, the trauma, the cold, the heat, the anger, the eggshells that I continue to walk on and away from.

Like a box, packed up and put to the curb.

Nothing has meaning until it's gone.

Though gone, it's never forgotten.

Because history lives on even when you put it to past.

It's the hope inside that you wished to change.

The "potential" that you fucked to get over the ex-moment, just to remind you why you missed "it" in the first place.

As I fold up everything in my space, I stop to rewind

I unfold each item one by one and lie upon my bed of insecurities praying.

Fear, the motherfucker that cheats you out of living.

But good Karma is the bitch that wears the 6 inch heels pressed into its neck.

The universe ultimately wins, returning back all the love I gave.

Its time, a new horizon to celebrate,

A new wall to commemorate, a new room to consummate.

But nothing feels as good as the old, until the new has come along.

I look around this room full of material things but still seem to be empty.

These walls hold best kept secrets

If they talked, they would only mumble just to be noticed, but not heard.

Ascension

Testing my patience.

Anxious Annie, always running to and never from.

Let the halos surrounding me keep my lights on while I'm running in the dark.

Unafraid of the journey to be,

Eyes closed because I just wanna feel free.

Let my good vibrations lead the way.

On my way to my big bubble of bliss.

In between Saturn and Mercury

Karma ruling over communications.

Flying without wings,

Making it look easier than it ever seems.

Tripped on a cloud today,

Looked behind me in the hazy reflection.

Let a tear drop for the old me, no longer here to be.

Finally got through to the light,

Let's toast this champagne to the new me.

She's perfectly imperfect, yet free.

Spreading love and peace to those in need.

High on life,

Appreciation of a sometimes-unwanted luxury.

Good karma never misses a beat.

Showering my soul with kisses, blessing me endlessly.

Smiles appeared through the darkness and laughter commenced through the sunrise.

Made it to the beginning,

Starting over again,

Complex Simplicity,

No cares,

Bumping Aiko in my eardrums,

Lost in the lyrics,

It's a real Trip.

The End of HER

I wanna go,

Far from pain,

Far from judgment,

Or from where I'm taken in vain.

Running from the old HER.

Feet clings to grass,

Running pass trees,

I'm glowing up,

All I see is green.

It's never what it seems,

Life is but a dream.

Longing for white picket fences,

A child-like vision,

Eyes pierced into the future,

The present doesn't fit the picture.

Shots fired,

Get down.

You've been robbed,

Grow up now,

Glow up now,

No more fantasy,

No more mommy,

No more daddy,

No more pacifier,

I am here to take you higher.

Elevate,

No more sweet escapes,

Only jig sawed puzzles,

A thousand pieces to put together,

All alone,

No other players,

Start it over,

Concentrate,

Work hard,

Fuck it up,

Repeat.

Lost in mother nature,

Searching for a new galaxy,

I am not human,

I am OTHER,

I am bold,

I am lost,

I am found,

I am right,

I am wrong,

I am me,

I am you,

I am LOVE.

I am One.

Where did she go?

On my heels,

Now vanished in the background,

Sounds of the wind blowing pass me,

Feet cold and wet,

Naked in the wild.

She won't ever understand.

This is my freedom.

Crying tears of joy,

Laughing hysterically,

Spinning around in circles,

Infinity,

Sun beams down,

Butterflies circling,

This is home.

Looking up above,

Peace.

Full Moon

There's something about the moon tonight.

Distant,

Like a lover who hasn't returned calls in a week.

It used to be just right,

Summer nights grooving,

to some ol'skool in the drop top.

Something is missing

like the diamond,

that once appeared brightly lit in photographs.

Abandoned by its owner,

But never wanting to part ways.

Full and gloomy

Beside misty clouds

Barely spotted,

a piece of crumb,

on dark carpet.

Swept away,

in a non-disclosed corner,

Just to satisfy a mother's

Compulsive disorder.

This night is deserving,

Pound cake and butter pecan ice cream,

After hours of slaving over a hot stove.

Deliciously perfect,

But end up bad for the tummy.

Stepping into a new night,

Afraid of what to endure,

Predators hiding behind dark shadows,

Awaiting the weak.

Alcoholic beverages,

turning two strangers into lovers overnight.

Screams of agony coming from the corridors.

Stains of red splashed on dingy walls.

Nosey neighbors keep quiet behind unsteel doors.

A runner's run cut short,

Horns beeping a mile away,

Bumpers touching each other,

Like Caribbean girls wining hips on one another at carnival.

Sweat secretes,

Pores smells of rum,

Friction heightens sensitivity.

On this night,

Incoming calls come in,

From unexpected past lovers.

Seeking lust,

Through nostalgic lenses,

Wanting more familiarity.

Selfishly addicted,

To more than just one hit,

Veins plucked by tight rubber bands,

Shooting up,

Achieving euphoric moments,

An impossible high.

Exploring,

Under a full moon.

Deliver

Head hung low,

Smile crooked,

Knees weak,

Words seen,

but unable to speak.

Sweet mumbles,

Jotted down in formation.

Heart beats to every stroke.

Pop,

Crackle,

Snap.

Go.set.READY.

Backwards thinking.

But Action speaks.

Even without verbalizing.

Pen to page.

Woke to fear.

Push.

Now I think I'm there.

Found in between lines.

Emerging from shallowed waters.

Dipped in gold,

Like the life I'm living.

Released, Out to

the universe,

A jittered wait.

No response.

But received.

Acknowledged by silenced mention.

Read the mask.

Told its soul.

Never to be spoken.

But instead felt,

With subtlety,

Ease and passivity.

Dancing around,

Aimlessly caught.

In denial,

In the now.

On the spot.

Can't stop looking at the clock.

My heart's pastime.

Hold close,

Open up,

Pull through.

Deliver.

But I don't know if my words reached you.

Chapter 4: New Beginnings

I choose the latter

The greater of us two.

You and I are one in the same.

With you I feel, I have instinct and I live through.

Every breath of me is a great indication of who you are deep down inside.

You come alive through music, dance, love, shared intimacy and life changing occurrences.

You are my heart's companion and you're so full of life.

You dance for my heart's beat and you rest assured of its happiness.

Nothing is as it seems.

They don't see you for you because I don't let them enter.

Made a few mistakes with you, shared you with darkness.

But now I only expose you to light.

When I met my soul......mate

I think I met him,

Matter of fact I know I did,

Through the waves of frequency,

We connected on a higher being,

It took me to notice myself before I noticed him.

My reflection,

He was.

He was sent to teach me,

Correcting my bad habits and mirroring them.

I saw myself within his smile

and his argumentative demeanor.

I was on a mission of discovery,

We never pollinated,

But he watched me turn Queen bee,

Leading a generation of lost to sweet honey.

His admiration led me to my frustration.

I knew him to be king,

But he wasn't ready.

Still being familiar with unfamiliar princesses.

He sung me his life with his sweet voice,

Serenaded by his wisdom,

His senses delved into mine,

Touch couldn't be replaced.

I was in it.

Energy lifted,

Compatible vibration,

Late night conversation,

So enticed, but never gave into temptation.

I wanted him to be greater,

But I needed to be great too.

So I left to fulfill my own,

Elevation.

Its hurts,

I had to let go.

So he can get right,

And find his kingdom within.

But this may not be the end.

We shall meet in the next life.

When we are both complete.

Revelation

Maybe I missed the signs.

Maybe you were right,

Before my eyes,

Before I made that left,

Turn into,

The Crooked lines,

Hazy eyes,

Hard to read between.

Reflections,

Objects in the mirror,

are closer than they seem.

GPS re-routed me in the aligned direction.

Was lost in translation,

Time wasted in wonderland.

All that glittered didn't glow,

But your presence,

Gently kissed my soul.

One heartbreak and disappointment at a time.

Patiently in the cut,

You lay,

Heart on pause,

Mind on me,

Eyes on prize,

Knelt down at my roots.

Watered my garden daily,

You helped cultivate the flowers,

that finally bloomed.

This is the season of reaping,

And you sow it all.

Ready, aim, shoot

No need to hide,

Angel guides shot me,

off my high horse.

No ego wherever we go.

Fell into your heart,

Hold me tight,

Love me up.

Reciprocation is my duty.

Sorry I missed you early on,

I promise to never,

leave a moment untouched.

Take my hand,

under this full moon.

Let our love,

illuminate the dark skies.

Climax full of butterflies,

Our hearts bond together,

With child-like smiles and perfect wonder.

The Miseducation

Stuck,

But the door is in front of me

Not sure if it's the beginning or the end for me.

Complacency got the best of me.

I pray the time just waits for me.

They say age is a factor, but I ain't letting it affect me.

Gonna do what I do and don't care who's doubting me.

Or maybe it's me doubting me,

Cuz I'm blinded by the unseen and too down to see the foreseen.

It only seems,

Life is but a dream.

I close my eyes and visualize,

In hopes that I realize,

It takes real eyes,

to look up even in the moment of the demise.

They rather see me cry than to see me alive.

Put my light on just so they could see me shine.

But I'm different, so they only wanna see me in the dark.

And I stay there hidden with wisdom in my heart.

Afraid of my potential, scared it may be all that my dreams were made of.

I don't want them to see me shine, they'll wish me bad when all I wanna do is survive.

Suppressing God's gift because I want them to be comfortable.

Want them to all to love me, even if it's a false interpretation.

Hoping their stares don't lead to my suffocation.

Trying to learn to be myself, but I drop out sometimes.

Blame it on my miseducation.

Support missing from my childhood memories.

Verbal miscommunications led me to my trepidation.

It's all love at the end though because I'm learning that I am my own enemy.

Singing a song like Rapsody,

"Been searching for myself and I ain't find shit".

Made a left turn at the corner and stepped in some shit.

Years later and the smell still on my consciousness.

Wanna do better, but the devil always starting with me.

Weighing him and my angel on my shoulders heavily,

like yin and yang.

Finally learning that all I need in life is just some balance.

Walking on a thin line, my footing ain't right,

Fell a few times so I left it alone til' the morning.

Morning turned into nights and into days that never persisted.

On to another lesson but I skipped class again.

Never ending cycle of finding me again.

My spirit is worn and I just wanna cheer her up one time for goodness sake.

I'm tired lord, please show me which route I should take.

I don't know how to do it,

Just get through it,

I'm not the smoothest,

Dizzy, on another planet,

Not from here,

Too green for this,

Too honest to dismiss.

In a game with sharks,

Heart bloody torn,

Awaiting a different outcome.

I am Woman

I am woman,

Filled with love and pride.

Nurturing to those who come behind me.

I stand for truth , so don't go believing lies.

I remember the night crawling down on my knees.

Waiting for an answer, screaming "Oh lord why me?"

The reason for me being here to speak, isn't because I fell down and became weak.

A stronger person was within me, had to let go of the negative energy.

Refuel my soul with love and understanding.

Sage my spirit,

Renew my heart,

Re-program my mind,

Surround my life with positivity

Last but not least,

Learn that I am not the enemy.

My soul will no longer be taxed.

For I will always remain queen.

Even through bondage, I will be

The Goddess that my ancestors taught me to be.

Never afraid because fear doesn't exist.

I'll rise up even when obstacles persist.

This is my life and only I can walk the shoes I live in.

I may get down, I may have frowned, may have stumbled upon a few unworthy of my good heart.

But I never gave up.

Never gave up on the good in this cold world.

Never gave up on true love, because it exists in my heart.

And though there aren't many like me,

I know there are some with the same good energy.

Threw out the bad apples, tarnishing my well being.

Cuz I know now that beauty is worth more than just seeing.

The eyes lie, but the soul sees clearly.

Blinded by affections, just to realize all along I was neglecting,

Me, myself and I

No this isn't selfish, nor an arrogant plea.

Just a note to self that in order to love someone I had to reach inside and learn to love all of me.

Stared at her in the reflection today,

Eyes filled with pain from baggage dragged from yesterday.

Breathed life into her,

Baby girl,

It's gonna be okay.

Cuz the sun's gonna shine

Just as bright as you are.

So let's get you out of the darkness.

And fill the world with this beauty we possess.

Chapter 5: Feels

There's no more clouds to chase.

I'm running out of options

Maybe I should stay put.

And let the clouds move towards me,

Look up in amazement and let them shower their love onto me.

The grass is colder on this side- I opt for hard concrete.

Discovering the many ways,

They could move without me.

Much like lovers.

Oh the clouds keep on running and I can't enjoy the sunshine.

Please slow down for me.

I really want to be.

Lost in serenity.

Lost and Unfound

Maybe me being found is forbidden

Cold and naked in this garden of fools

Universal laws keep you hidden

It's raining and I need you soon.

Wrap your warmth around me,

Sweet lips brushed upon my cheeks.

Tell me the truth with your eyes

Hearts surrender to divine timing.

Time doesn't exist in 5D, so let's take this down two notches.

Biologically, we're running out of it.

Let's have these memories while were young.

Make this feel like 90s Brooklyn Summer at the block party.

I wanna dance with you;

Bright smiles, dreamy eyes as we manifest love under Scorpio's full moon.

Wishes come into fruition when the afterthought is gone.

You appear effortlessly massaging my every worry into bliss.

Nothing can measure up to your immense care and soft kiss.

Even when I doubt it's you,

All of my misfits, are beauty in your eyes.

Kiss me when I'm emotional, laugh at my random outbursts.

Call me beautiful, when I'm batshit crazy.

Take my hand across the ocean and spark a blunt in the midst of live jazz melodies. Take care of my heart and my home;

Never too much for you to handle.

Soft cuddles, tingling hearts, butterflies and chills up my spine.

All the signs saying you're indeed mine.

My Mine

Been dreaming again, well I fell in a fantasy.

It was sunny and beautiful,

All white everything.

We lived in a modest home outside of the country.

All we had was love.

All we had was peace.

All we had was joy.

All we had was US.

You ran away with me,

Across many moons,

Just to make love reign,

I never wanted anything more,

You helped set me free.

To let go and be,

The beautiful manifestation, That God wanted me to be.

All we had was love.

All we had was time.

All we had was God.

All we had was US.

You made sure my every need was met.

Never had to ask for anything,

Because, you created happiness.

Never told me No,

Kept on loving me,

Unconditionally.

You taught me well.

You taught me patience.

You taught me trust.

You taught me kindness.

You taught me love.

How did you put the awe in awesome?

Came out the blue,

My world turned upside down,

But you still managed to hold me down

Lucky you to experience this with me.

Two peas, one pod.

Always ready for the ride.

Beautiful chaos,

Blessings in disguise.

Out of the dark,

Flashing the light.

Capture my every essence,

Notice my every beautiful

Even when I cry because I feel ugly.

Pick me up like I never left.

Wake up to my sweet kisses.

And know that I got nothing but love for you.

Still.

Though my mind leaves me off track, you always seem to reel me back.

You had me, even when everyone turned their backs.

Even when your back was against the wall.

You always saw through me.

I never knew what it was you saw.

Seeing you in awe, made me feel seen.

But I was blind.

And you took your time to teach me.

Something New

Out of the blue,

A ribbon in the sky,

Sweetest taboo,

Every time I'm with you.

No pressure,

Simply pleasure,

Adorning me.

Lips taste so sweet,

Dipped in backwoods' tips.

I taste the smoke.

Shotgun,

Take my breath away.

Not afraid of my tears or misfits.

Comfort me in the face of it all.

Brushing past my anxiety just to get closer to you.

Our song is playing every time you're in the room.

Never stop smiling when I'm with you.

There's never uncertainty about the truth.

Never knew this could be true,

Wished upon the 11:11 stars

And stumbled upon you.

But how do you do what you do?

In my own bubble,

Come meet me across the moon.

Let my hair down,

Run your hands down my back,

Let these good vibrations light up the sack.

Staring into your eyes,

I urge to run from it all, but something pulls me closer.

Maybe it's that pretty smile, the way that you hold me, the way that you stare, the way that you care.

Kryptonite to my cool, because I'm clueless with you.

Giggles and smiles,

Stumbles and trips,

Stubbornness and then came the fall.

Every step of the way you're right there,

To catch me throughout it all.

Sister (Emmy's Pain)

Dark clouds hang over my head

But all they see is the sun shining

It gets lonely in here

A dark hole,

Where's the light?

I can't seem to find it.

Lost between the dirty and the good fight.

No one seemed to look through me

They only looked with shaming eyes

Judging my very existence

All because I was born to be different

No friends in sight,

Just strangers who are broken

Hurt masked by their popularity

Their egos trampled over my sanity.

But I am a princess,

a peaceful warrior is all they know of me.

Took my kindness for fool.

But my heart is strong and my spirit lives on.

I stare at my empty reflection

Searching for answers. No one to talk to

So my burdens thickens.

Pray is what they tell me to do

I try and get lost in context clues

I don't think he hears me,

Slept in Satan's lair

Cut off from all five senses.

So I couldn't make sense of it.

Maybe God called for me before I descended

But I was already deaf ears and blinded eyes to the light.

I heard them calling me,

It got a little fuzzy

The special vitamin that the nurse administered

On my tongue, mouth shut, 8oz water floating down my throat.

Thirty minutes in

I'm numb to the pain

Slightly delusional

A loss of EQ

Artificial Intelligence

Takes over

I'm stuck

But they just see me groggy

I'm high

But into my lower self

I can't escape and pain dwells

Like four walls, no doors, no windows Tied up and stripped of all.

Insane Asylum

But I see you there by my side

Trying your hardest

So I crack a simple smile

Because your presence is worth it

Though I can't feel you

My soul remembers love

But this second dose makes me forget how it feels.

Then I'm back in my dear melancholy

Fighting the thoughts with prayers that seem to always go unanswered.

I want you to save me, but I can't scream

It will only make me seem more crazy

So I cry a river

Hoping you step into a puddle of it

Get your feet wet in my sorrow

A day in my shoes

You couldn't fathom

But I get your purpose.

Far from insane, close to falling

Trapped in darkness,

Awaiting prayers to be answered

So that there may be light.

This tunnel is long and I can't see

Past the walls that forbid me.

Chapter 6: Missing Parts

Sweet Shiraz

Never a dull moment when I'm home

All alone, but never feeling it.

A long day of work has got to end with ease.

Shower sprays hard on my flesh,

Suds covering my imperfections.

Natural kinks curl up at the touch of the wetness.

Face drowned with streams of tears,

Hadn't done it in a while.

All cried out,

So, I hop out, towel in tow.

Drying,

Wrapped around my belly.

Coconut oil caresses every inch of my body.

Pure silk.

I run to my sweet red,

Twist her top off,

Pour her,

Half full is how I see her.

One sip of the sweetest bitch.

Heavens shined as I bumped that 90's R&B and sipped.

Lips pierced as the lip gloss stains etched into the glass.

Rich and warm goodness.

Just me and sweet Shiraz,

Never disappoints.

Always on point.

I sip and sing.

Into another time zone, back to future.

Bold Shiraz,

You always know what I need.

Hold my lips in contempt.

Sniff, swirl and taste,

My kind of red.

Not the type that brings me pain,

But the one that helps me endure.

Glass half empty,

I want more.

Fill my cup,

Fill this void

Make me smile,

Make me numb,

I wanna dance,

Make me go dumb,

Text my friends I love em'

Curse out the dumb fuck who canceled our fuck.

Now I'm fucked,

But you never left my side.

Fine Shiraz, My ride or die.

With you I seek and hide

Searching for my soul,

Hiding my insecurities.

Feeling high off life.

Teedra blasting through my speakers.

I just wanna be happy,

Free from the bs,

When I'm with you.

You help release endorphins on a late night.

I rather be hugging this full glass of you than to only receive half of him.

You take me,

You taste me,

You heard me,

You love me.

You and I.

Until the fuckboys fuck off.

And a real man steps up.

Just me and my sweet Shiraz.

Just me and my bitch.

The Fall

I never knew what it was or even how to receive.

A cold heart, hidden in the dark, slow to touch; hard to believe.

Infatuations clouded my mind, falling for potential, never amounting to anything.

Hopeless Romance left with no hope or a chance.

Genuine hearts usually cry in the shadows of pretty bright smiles.

Exhausted by the cycle of deceit,

Who said it conquered all?

Never knew it for it to come and defeat.

Scars not shown, hurt me till we make-up;

My face drawing on an empty care.

Through it all, I still believe.

It will find me.

Through the bloody massacre happening internally,

Chasing me through the hallowed woods,

Rushing past amazon trees,

Jumping into the lake,

Swimming past the shore,

Back strokes,

Deep diving,

Just to capture me.

Heart shivering,

Eyes never seen,

Skin never felt,

Lips never parted,

Legs steady trembling,

Hands slowly risen to the sky.

Holding me in contempt,

Tapped out,

Effortlessly.

Intertwines into my soul.

A rich lather glued;

The universe spoke aloud,

And right then I knew.

Tag, You're it.

Broken Mirror

I don't know what to say when you read me that way.

Put my flaws on the table and shuffled them in your hands.

Dealt me a scary one,

Forced me to see;

while all along comforting me.

Took off my blindfold;

Your eyes were the mirror to my actions,

Your voice held conviction and love;

Gaining my soul's attention.

Felt immensely,

Wake up call to my reality.

You pushed me.

And I was reluctant,

Ego in the way of my growing.

I lay bare,

As you whisper naked truths to my stubborn spirit.

Turning the other cheek,

But your hand softly pulls me closer,

Eyes tell a sweet story as they stare into mine.

Your words gave me strength.

Caressed my soul and kissed my heart,

Fed my mind and shivered through my body.

And right then I knew

All along it was you.

Loner

Facing my fears,

With a face full of tears,

Finding a way but I know I can't stay,

Was down for the ride,

But feelings can't hide.

The fact that it's real and killing me inside.

Burst all the bubbles,

Put it to shame,

When they say I'm the one that got away,

They shake their heads when mentioning my name.

Their thoughts ring like echoes,

Stinging my ears,

Suddenly their lies reappear.

Into my phone,

While I'm alone,

Throw them a bone,

Then they go home.

I'm cold and naked,

No one to cover me.

Water filled eyes,

Meet their demise.

I can't deny the void I suppress,

That turns me into a big ol' mess,

Not looking for saviors,

Just looking for peace.

Can't seem to find it here within me.

I runaway, just to escape.

Thoughts aloud, always insane.

Light the candles, burn the sage,

But first let me get through this;

undeniable rage.

Let me find darkness,

And there I'll find light.

To keep me going and win the good fight.

Heart on my sleeve and they take it and run.

Just another girl on the IRT;

The gullible one.

No one to trust,

No one to wash the ache.

Soul bound to its very last tear.

End of the rope,

Questioning if I belong.

But the fight keeps me,

And fear keeps me from sleep.

Awakening my dreams and manifesting my new reality.

Chapter 7: The Finale

Who are you?

A question I ask my reflection daily.

Staring at a stranger with a smile that brings us closer.

I think I know you or maybe knew,

From your soft afro, like Egyptian cotton, to your deep dimples that hold sacred dreams.

I see your beauty, past the curve of your lips down to your lovely brown skin.

Your eyes tell a story, and a dream unfolds.

Smile carries pain and perseverance,

Heart sings of joy that overcame.

Mind screams thoughts that dance anxiously.

You are love.

Where I Wanna Be

Where should I start?

Show me the way,

Don't let my indiscretions lead to your escape.

Speak up, help elevate us to another level of space,

Or is it time that you need?

Eagerness tearing us apart.

Hand full with a piece of my heart,

But you don't see the shards that keeps it bleeding.

Put it in your front pocket, over your chest.

Hold it when you need warmth and want to feel my presence.

Smiles and laughs mask the lonely.

Tight hugs and sweet kisses to ease the pain.

But your returns are sometimes in vain.

Emotions less, con fusions

Tiptoeing around the shells of an egg that's already been cracked. Too stubborn to pick up the pieces.

Crying more under full moon nights

Praying my intentions manifested right.

Wrong is all I knew, until I met you.

See right through my walls and cheery disposition.

Don't want me to hurt more, so you feel lost in your position.

Co-dependency issues causing big friction.

Hating on my flaws, feeling like I failed the mission.

But then you come out of nowhere and show me more than I fell for in the movies.

Rom-coms depicting how It should be, Envious of fictitious characters,

Face to face with my reality.

Tired of running away,

So I accepted being with you.

Appreciation of a good-hearted black man, Respect is what I have for you,

On top of the love poured into.

Willing to stick around,

Even through the intermissions.

The show will always go on,

Even when the curtain closes and the masks are hung up on the mirror.

I see the beauty in the reflection.

Here goes my luggage,

And you unpack it patiently with me.

Giving me a chance to just be.

I know it is a lot, but I am not.

Apology.

Death to Ego

Life never tells you the hows, nor the whens and wheres.

Not giving a fuck about the who's or what happened and we barely get a why.

Why did this have to happen to us during this time?

And how can so many of us die?

What the fuck is going on? And Who the fuck is doing this?

I know you heard my screech in the wees of darkness.

Weeping to settle the sorrow,

Hoping to get a chance at seeing another tomorrow.

Then regret it in the evening when the drip falls from the bottle. But what is good in a world full of greed?

Soul surviving on a backed up generator,

Sponsored by my ancestors.

I feel the pull and the push,

Ready to deliver,

But it's breeched.

Head still in the belly of lies.

One foot out,

And my cries murmured through thick mucus walls.

Yet no one hears me.

Heavy foot on the gas.

On my way to hang mountainside.

Let the demons take over the cliff, Spirit guides catch me before the fall.

My ego won't let me go.

Should I go?

The bottom seems up, when you're looking from beneath.

Self-Talk

A time or two or maybe three,

I look at you in the reflection,

Those lips, that smile those hips.

All in sync with your big personality.

But personally, it's your heart that leaps forward to hug.

It's your soul that glows and brings forth cheer.

Out of your mind, so focused, yet discombobulated.

Your kisses hold the sweetest sugar.

Made from universe's secret blessings.

Can't be bought but will be earned.

Your passion runs deep, so intricate, and free.

Yet no one knows the real she,

Beauty blinded by anxiety, off beat, in your own rhythm.

Yet with just a blink of an eye you stay killin' em' softly,

Pretty smile and light that forever shines.

Never trying too hard,

Had a few heartbreaks and misfortunes but you bounced back like Spalding.

If only they knew, the testimony that led to this harmony.

How the universe keeps on blessing you like royalty.

Divine Time

Prayers went up

And love was found.

Though it never left,

Just magnified.

I didn't have to lose me,

To be with you.

 With God on our side,

Winning is inevitable.

Even if the future looks murky,

One look in your eyes,

And I feel the possible arise.

Your faith never wavered,

The ribbon still in the sky.

A reminder that love is never to be done,

But to be and experienced unconditionally.

We are both deserving.

Both delivered the same blessing, Why did he choose us to fly?

With broken wings,

We persevere through the night,

Chasing the full moon.

Manifesting love with just our beaming hearts.

Beats the same rhythm,

Unspoken mentions,

Just thankful for this perfect picture.

Framed by God's adorning hands,

Crafted in his grace,

Founded in his mercy,

Gifted in his love.

Goodbyes are Forever

Farewell to the whens, wheres, hows and whys of yesterday.

Grand Rising to the whats and what nots of today.

Headed down the road of mystery, learning that those who were supposed to be; are simply enemies.

Got me looking at the inner me, like maybe it's all on me.

The problem child that arises with no solution in sight. Pulled the strings from my chest,

Let the aches echo the gory vicinity.

Now ask me if it's worth it.

A world full of preconceived notions.

Got me thinking I don't know shit.

But who really does know anything?

A man that knows, know not at all.

Maybe this is why I sit short of my fall.

Waiting for the leaves to fly off trees,

The colors turn in front of me,

Let the wind blow away this toxicity,

Birds flying high, mimicking the best of me.

It feels like when Judas betrayed Jesus, but ain't no forgiving

I feel like I know why the blue caged bird sings

I feel like I'm alone, walking towards my evolution.

Feet scorched from the long walks in desert sands, hours from parting the red seas.

I feel like the ugly duckling is finally becoming the swan.

I feel like you should leave me alone. After all was done, all was said

All that left this relationship undone.

Done in my eyes but not in my heart.

Feeling of failure and it's all on me.

We're just victims of our egos getting the best of us.

Or could it just be me?

All Said, All Done

Love unrequited,

Never been one,

Nothing to be reunited.

Shattered glass,

When it wasn't returned.

You played,

Put your love on layaway.

I put up the payments,

But never could get it out.

Staring at the receipts,

I guess time doesn't love me.

I can't afford this bill,

But I afforded the mess it came along with.

Loving my non-existent counterparts.

Potential can only bare for so long,

Then the real person shows up.

Smiles of deceit, body of lust, mouth of lies, whispers of sweet nothings.

Pedestal higher than your ego,

Surpasses my love for me.

Spirit crying in the dark,

Observing the trampling of a pure heart.

Leopards never change their spots,

You wouldn't sacrifice being right to be in harmony.

Wanted me subservient to your flaws even if affected me.

I am not happy, I am trapped and need to get off this merry-go round.

Our toxicity isn't safe for either of us.

I can't stay, my path no longer lies here.

The lesson is the start of my new-found blessings.

Not about you, this is all on me.

Time to move on and put me up first.

I Release your bond to open my heart up anew.

Let love conquer and fill me up.

Let it reign through my heart with sincerity and break down walls patiently to get through the unseen.

Beautiful souls intertwine in sync, ordained from above.

A mutual understanding of love.

Let's face it, sometimes love just plain sucks! It can make you act completely crazy, cause crippling self-doubt, and riddle you with issues of abysmal self-worth and general less-thannothing-ness. But, when done right – focusing on self-love, above all else, (plus putting the time and effort into self-reflection, and forward progression) it just might pleasantly surprise you! Join poet Indigeaux Sol as she guides you along her own tumultuous journey through the ups and downs of love. Delight as she feverishly weaves her way through the often murky waters of love-spurned self-discovery, and goes from feeling worthless, to on top of the world, and ultimately, to achieving the most beautiful love of all. Told through skillfully-crafted poetry and prose, Prelude to Love is a must-read for any lover of poetry, and likewise, any lover of love.

Indigeaux is a multifaceted creator who hails from Brooklyn, NY. She has always possessed a love for writing, and especially poetry, since she was a child – utilizing it, even at a young age, as an outlet to release her bottled up emotions. She now uses her writing to help uplift women and tell stories that are relatable, and helpful for self-healing. Indigeaux graduated with honors

from City College of New York, where she earned her bachelor's degree in Creative Writing and

Journalism. She enjoys a career as a Freelance Marketing Consultant, and pursues her other passions as a podcaster, performing artist, plus-size model, and songwriter. Indigeaux is now

embarking on her newest endeavor, launching her creative production company, Indigeaux Sol Cre8s. She currently resides in South Carolina, but is always on the lookout for a new place to fulfill her life's journey.

Made in the USA
Middletown, DE
25 February 2022

61805698R00073